Seasons of Light

Seasons of Light

*Poems & Ekphrasis Poems
by
Bonny Barry Sanders*

Cherry Grove Collections
Cincinnati

*All the best to you,
Bonny*

© 2024 by Bonny Barry Sanders

Published by Cherry Grove Collections
P.O. Box 541106
Cincinnati, OH 45254-1106

ISBN: 9781625494481

Poetry Editor: Kevin Walzer
Business Editor: Lori Jareo

Visit us on the web at www.cherry-grove.com

Author photo by Cathie Trogdon

for my parents and brother, for the Hempsells, for all my friends and neighbors on Saltworks Creek and in Annapolis, and for all my friends and neighbors on Greenfield Creek and in Jacksonville

Acknowledgments

The author wishes to express grateful acknowledgment to the editors of the following magazines and journals in which these poems first appeared, a few in slightly different versions.

The Aurorean: "First Lessons"

Avocet: "Audience," "Reward," "I Come Away Knowing Everything but What Time It is," "We Had Almost Forgotten How"

Blueline: "Lulled to Sleep," "Never Give Away an Old Dog Dish," "New Reality," "Observation"

CALYX: A Journal of Art and Literature: "Blue Apricots"

Christian Century: "You Can Tell It's Fall"

The Christian Science Monitor: "Butterfly Garden," "Direction," "Where Nothing Speaks" (Original title: "Language"), "Orchestra-in-the-Round," "The Chuck-Will's-Widow," "The Purpose"

Ginger Hill: "Getting through It"

King's Estate Press: "Sonnet on Riding the Bus in New York City," (Original title: "Taking the Bus in New York City")

Louisiana Literature: "Color of Silk"

The Midwest Quarterly: "All These Comings and Sudden Goings," "Language of Wings," "Re-Invent What Life Gives You," "Like Love in the Afternoon"

Plainsongs: "Flutes of the Wood Thrush," "Forecasts," "Get Out of My Way," "Inherited," "Our Walks" (Original title: "Morning Walks")

Red Owl: "Rounding Sheep's Meadow"

Sun Times: "September Stroll through a Japanese Flower Market" (Original title: "From a Japanese Flower Market"), "June First"

Ekphrasis Poems

The Christian Science Monitor: "In Jan Van Eyck's *Portrait* of *Arnolfini and His Wife*,"

Kennebec: A Portfolio of Maine Writing: "The Color of His Language," "They Think I'm Deaf"

Louisiana Review: "The Mozart Sonata"

October House: "Over My Shoulder"

Poetry Motel: "Irises, 1889"

South Carolina Review: "What Ghiberti Knew"

For those who encouraged her in the compilation of this collection through its various stages, the author wishes to record her thanks. This includes the editorial advice of Janée Baugher and the technical assistance of Tim Norman.

Sincere gratitude goes to Denelle (Dani) Urbizu for her valuable support and the final formatting of the manuscript.

Contents

I.   Summer

Blue Apricots	17
What Is It We Celebrate?	18
Treasures	19
Re-invent What Life Gives You	20
I Come Away Knowing Everything but What Time It Is	22
I Saw a Clutch of Hatchlings Once	23
Bioluminescence	24
Not for Its Own Sake	25
Dilemma	26
Butterfly Garden	27
When You Go to a Butterfly Aviary	29
Language of Wings	31
First Trip Abroad	32
Color of Silk	33
Exotics	34
Red Begonia Summer	35
The Yellow Mandolin that Hangs on Our Living Room Wall	36
An Evening with the Syracuse Symphony	38
View from Aleyska Lodge, Alaska	40
Counting Memories	41
Where Nothing Speaks	42

II.   Autumn

You Can Tell It's Fall	45
Graceful Strings of White Wings	46
Foxes	48
Get Out of My Way	49
Riding the Bus in New York City	50
My Mother, the Actress	51
Playing and Singing the Old Songs became a Sweet Salve	53
Memorial Room	55
A Visit	56

Getting Through It	57
First Lessons	58
Private Piano Concert	59
Keeping the Jive	60
No Ghosts—only a Symphony of Sounds	61
Never Give Away an Old Dog Dish—	62
September Stroll through a Japanese Flower Market	63
Lulled to Sleep	65
The Way Land Invades Sky	66
Rounding Sheep's Meadow	67
Longleaf Pine on the Side of Our House	68
A Comparison	69

III.   Winter

New Reality	73
Into Winter Wind	74
Orchestra-in-the-Round	75
Direction	77
Up Harfield Trail to Robinhood Road	78
Observation	79
Audience	80
Iroquois Lodge	81
We Had Almost Forgotten How	82
Inherited	83
Snowbound	84
Faces in the Door	85
Why Take a Photo of an Old Goat House	86
Your Nourishing	87
The Purpose	88

IV.   Spring

Forecasts	91
The Chuck-Will's-Widow,	92
A Wet May Morning	93
Reward	94
Our Walks	95

June First	96
"Hello Susan," I Said to You	97
More than Déjà-vu	98
All These Comings and Sudden Goings	99
Sophie's Painting	100
"Way Down Upon the Swanee (sic) River"	101
Like Love in the Afternoon	102
Perfect Camouflage	103
Black Sleeve of Night	104
Symbiosis	105
Flutes of the Wood Thrush	106

V. Ekphrasis Poems

What Is Ekphrasis Poetry?	109
What Ghiberti Knew	110
The Mozart Sonata	112
Irises	113
Over My Shoulder	114
The Color of His Language	116
They Think I'm Deaf	117
In Jan Van Eyck's *Portrait of Arnolfini and His Wife*,	119
Pregnant Woman	120
A Painting for Bella, My Fiancée, My Love	121
Woman II, 1961	123
Mysterious Women	125
Ode on a Wedgewood Teapot	127
Notes about the Author	131

I. Summer

Blue Apricots

A departure of clouds—we watched
sky explode into the substance of opals.
Distant hills and nodding asters
under the fruit trees come into focus.
Apricots laid out to dry on yellow tablecloths
turn blue in the ripples of sun and shade under
the willow trees. On the tongue,
fruit azury to the taste.
Things most substantial
become suddenly ephemeral.

What Is It We Celebrate?

Is it not the roseate spoonbills that visit our cove?
They sein for fish, going in circles, scouring
the muddy bottom with their long flat bills—
all business, focused, occupied from sunrise to dusk.
I want to know if they found all they need
along the shoreline as they hurry
behind a school of fish, and where do they go
when sunset matches the color of their feathers.
And where is their secret rookery.

About tomorrow—nothing like my schedule.
No appointments, nothing to fix, no shopping.
They have built a nest, raised young already this year.
They will do it again next year. And the next.
And the next. They faithfully perform what the species
needs to survive—that inner knowing.
What else could one ask of them.
That is more than enough to celebrate.

Treasures

Hovering bony fingers
of red mangrove shelter us
from hard-violet rays.
Through emerald light, limestone reefs

grow into gentle humps—hammocks.
Close-up: jungle of sea grape,
sharp-toothed sedge, slash pines, palm.
Seeping-glow of sun breaks through

density spotlighting
air plants, glade lobelia,
buttonwood, a white egret on one leg
in water the color of dark rubies.

Black mangroves send breathing tubes
like brown cigars from their branches.
We forget sky until
boardwalk ends at West Lake.

Pink grasses bend low. Our gaze, adjusting to light,
lifts high into a mahogany hammock—
hundreds of white egrets dangling on branches
like large grapefruit,

and a gold swamp prairie
extending endlessly.
This is all the treasure Ponce de Leon
ever found in Florida.

Re-invent What Life Gives You

    Response to the advice from Naomi Shihab Nye
    in her poem "Valentine for Ernest Mann"

Dear Naomi Shihab Nye,

You asked me to let you know where
I found a poem. I checked my garage,
the odd sock in my drawer, deep in the dark
holes of my oldest shoes—all your suggestions.
And others besides. Finally I found the place—

in our salty creek. The first alligator I've seen
in five years conducted himself toward the headwaters.
(They don't like brackish water).
Not a sound. At first he was a log the tide
was carrying on its back up-stream by the pilings
where we saw three manatee last year. Double-take:

I saw the eyes—eyes that link millenniums,
colorless eyes in whose irises
stories wind like a vortex back, and further back.
Those eyes—cold calculators of caution, logical
constructs of awareness—they must have poems
residing in them like your skunks have.
The alligator probably read my thought.

I could have lost sight of him at any moment—
slick antecedent of the earliest submarines. I saw
the rich, rippled texture of his skin—no target now for shoes,
or belts, or purses. Yes, I could say he was beautiful—
but not really an apt subject
for a Valentine's poem, however. I must

hurry to warn my husband who loves to jump
into the deepest part of the creek to cool off
after he's cut the grass.

I Come Away Knowing Everything but What Time It Is

Far off the coast, I watch shrimp boats
        work the horizon where the color blue

is arabesque. Closer in, dolphins cascade
        from the envelope of the sea.

The tide has been washing
        and rinsing its wares,

and the waves will strew
        all the multi-colored,

calcium houses on the lap
        of the beach.

Time contracts as the wind drops
        its history in my ear.

I Saw a Clutch of Hatchlings Once

I would like to be there
when the clutch of sea turtle eggs
break the crisp cells they have been stored in
for 60 days and their frontal flippers dig up
through six feet of sand, leave shredded shells
behind them, and make the sand's surface churn
and boil. When the flat paws of their hind flippers
squeak as they drag down the beach.

I wonder what will wake them—the heat of noonday,
or the gibbous moon, heavy in her pregnancy,
hovering over the nests, warming the night to just
the right temperature, when she will guide the turtles
to the sea, hurrying them along. Or will the lights
from the homes, condos, and businesses misdirect them,
or will raccoons, dogs, foxes find them?

I saw a clutch of hatchlings once churn the sand
and sprint for the ocean. One wandered off. My niece
carried him back on track and set him waterborne.
The Turtle Patrol posted a notice: "Eggs from Nest 34
Expected to hatch July 24." It will be the day when 100 pairs
of frontal flippers will span the sea, their new home.
I keep checking— I want to witness this marvel again,
feel the connection, when the sea accepts
another gift from the shore.

Bioluminescence

I look for evidence, fragments of memory come—
There was the effect of sun once on the wind-rippled,
moving surface of our protected cove.
Waves washing in, tide pulling out,
Wind moving over it like a brush, lights glinting
silver like millions of mica chips.
You pointed it out to me, the wonder in your eyes.

Our fishermen's boots. The winter beach
lined with ice crystals and snow,
moon reflecting its crescent form on the wet sand, our boots
stirring up the phosphorus jellyfish—we called them—
in the shallow, icy water along the shore. Bioluminescence—
jellies, the size of one's little fingernail. In summer
we'd see their glow at night in the water boiling up
behind the motor of our boat—sea sparkle,
single celled plankton emitting their light.

I look for more evidence, fragments of light. The fireflies
those summer nights on their journeys up
into the highest trees when I lay my head in your lap.
We counted hem together.
Yes, all the smiles that lit your face.

Not for Its Own Sake

There's no end to tending my garden—
azaleas, pentas, impatience, begonias, ivy.
I can never say, "There, that's it.
It's done. I'm finished."
Every year there's the planting.
Every month there's the pruning.
Every week there's the weeding and watering.

Not that the garden doesn't give back to me.
Not that it demands attention
for its own sake, but that its want
supplies my need—the deep-rooted
desire to nourish, to connect.

Dilemma

Honeysuckle vines
    cover the full, bushy juniper
      by my mailbox.

The fragrant vine
   will soon strangle
     the evergreen.

But honeysuckle blossoms
  are food
    for the swallowtail,

the monarch,
   the red-spotted purple.
     I call this *sacrifice*.

Gardens are famous
  for one sort of denial
    or another.

Butterfly Garden

1.
I bought plants just for the butterflies:
sage, mint, dill, parsley, heliotrope, fennel,
some hibiscus, pentas, impatiens,
and stalky blue statice for line and color,
oriental grass for texture.

I found boards from a neighbor's toss-out pile,
sand from the exposed hill, a layer
of clippings and leaves from the yard, black
dirt from new construction down the road—
I could salvage that.

No one would be startled at my sighs,
at least I can try to give
back to the earth, replenish the habitat
(small price for such restoration).

2.
It's the third day I've noticed
a tiger swallowtail
bouncing on wind gusts around
the corner of the house
testing the gardenias, then the hibiscus.
He catches the scent of the rich, pink pentas
and pulls out long drafts,
his wings tipping
together to strengthen the pull,
his abdomen pointing to the sun
like a gnomon.

I know it's the same swallowtail
tasting my resolve to give
this small patch back to the earth.

When You Go to a Butterfly Aviary

Don't go on a weekend when everyone is there.
Don't go on a Monday when it might be closed.
Check. Go with a very quiet person or no one at all.
Go early because you might want to stay all day.
Take lunch and a book with a bright cover.

When you enter the humid tropical forest of flowers,
mist will rise and you might feel vapor embrace you slightly.
That will pass. You will hear the faint swish
of a little stream sounding like organdy skirts
of girls dancing. Beds of impatiens are bordered with rocks.
Then you might feel a small wind on your cheek.
It will be from the indigo wings of a hairstreak as it passes you.
Sit for a long time on a bench and pretend you are reading
your book. All the time you will be watching
a zebra swallowtail feeding on an apple slice.
Its wings opening and closing softly like eyelids.
Continue to sit still and pretend to read but keep watching.
A monarch might land on your book, attracted
by its color or on your sleeve, or on the visor of your cap.
Maybe on your glasses. A long-tailed skipper
might sit for a long time on your collar
and read over your shoulder. Don't move.

You will begin to feel the faux rainforest pulling you in.
Now you'll notice hundreds of silvery blues
down by the little stream and many varieties
resting camouflaged against branches and undersides
of leaves so they look like a leaf themselves.

Many will be high up along the screens.
Some will be hunched along branches
lined up like starlings on telegraph wires.
Others will be perched on a lily pad,
their wings folded together so they look like
a tiny fleet of sailboats. Even the rainbow
does not have so many colors as you will see from your bench.
Nothing will intrude. The sounds of the rainforest—
water rushing, mist seeping through small holes in hidden
pipes, birds chirping, rain dripping from trees—
will block out noises from the street.

Time now to pull out your sandwich, break off a corner,
set it beside you on the railing—you might have a guest.
A juicy piece of fruit can certainly bring in a colorful
common morpho. It may take hours
to experience all this natural beauty,
because you have entered a different world.
You are the guest of a fragile place of light and color,
where time is not the dictator.

Language of Wings

What is this sun catcher
doing now. He's perched in air as if
he's on an invisible string, one end hung
from the garden post, the other from my chair.
His wings cut my morning's horizon
like origami scissors cut rice paper.
He just flew in from South America.
Does my English startle him?
There he goes sampling my menu—
impatiens, red hibiscus, blue plumbago.
His day rotates on a bright flurry
of motion like Calder's mobiles.
The whirring purr of his wings, my only warning.
He's all color like a Matisse.
He treads air while he reads the red
on my book cover, puts his wings in reverse,
scissors sheets of sun around him
into paper-thin shapes the way
my mother's slim shears cut through white satin,
hands nudged folds of glossy fabric
into waistline pleats, and fingers stitched
Alençon lace to the bodice of my wedding gown.
This sun-shimmering spanner of oceans
will return in a few months to his Latin tropics.
I wonder what language is spoken
where light took my mother?
It must be full of color—
vowels cut in the shape of splendor
                              like this bird.

First Trip Abroad

You were happy with the peppermint tea
and chocolate biscuits we bought
at the closet-size convenience store in Soho.
We heated the tea in our electric pot,
elevated our weary feet, and pretended we were home
sipping from your great-great grandmother's
hand-painted Limoges with green eucalyptus leaves.

After London, we headed north to pay respects
to D. H. Lawrence, the Brontës, Wordsworth.
Visited the homes of Shakespeare and Jane Austen
on the way south. Then we crossed the Channel,
touched the cold nudity of *Venus de Milo*,
stood with the hordes to photograph *Mona Lisa*.
You yawned accidently in the face
of the *Winged Victory of Samothrace*,
then we explored the Latin Quarter & Versailles.

We left a few things to do next time
but I knew we had seen it all
when the towering iron web of the Eiffel Tower
lit the night and defined the Eternal City as it defined us
while we sipped café au lait and dined on crepes
in les Jardin des Tuileries.
I saw you were at home in the world.

Color of Silk

> Summer in Bangalore, India

Bougainvillea blossoms fallen
in the night, carpet sidewalks
with fuchsia-colored tissues
that set the streets on fire
with morning's first light
before the street sweepers
in their bright silk sarees
with brooms made of small twigs
sweep them into piles
much as we discard
simple histories of our past—
delicate and distant.

Exotics

The green tree beside our cottage
is an orchestra tuning up, a rookery
for chattering, clamoring green parrots—
I mistake them for leaves. On our rooftop,

iridescent peacocks strut, necks
blazing green/blue, tail feathers fan out,
each with one large black eye.
They catch the sheen of the sun's lowering fire.

The outrageous pink of the bougainvillea
bleeds into the sunset like the last songs
he played on his guitar that merged into the years.
The concert from the green tree ends suddenly—

hundreds of birds silenced by advancing shadows.
One lone peacock's silhouette stands against deeply
damasked sky—soon to surrender to night
as I surrendered all those long ago songs.

Red Begonia Summer

    For Susan

I painted the deck chairs red
to go with the six red stripes
in our flag flying on the back of the wind
to welcome her home from London.
Red begonias at every turn—
new pots at the landing, the front door,
on the picnic table and side patio.
Every week I brought more flowers to plant
until all preparations
came together on the day
our daughter, gone so long,
walked through the front door past
all those red blossoms
and time stopped.

The Yellow Mandolin that Hangs on Our Living Room Wall

Strains of live orchestra music
floated over the water from the verandas
of the grand, old wooden hotels circling Fourth Lake.

Summer nights, my father hotel-hopped,
"I'd pick up vacationing city girls," he told us,
"in my grandfather's Adirondack canoe."

Loon calls, a warm evening, not out too deep, backrest
at a slant. Hotel lights wavering on the water.
Full moon. *"Whispering while you cuddle you near me…,"* *

Dad would croon on his Uncle Will's mandolin
as he strummed softly. He remembered all the chords
and fingering Uncle Will taught him.

Thirteen years now since his wife passed away,
he still remembers all the words,
sings them through the house as he works.

"Whispering why you'll never leave me,
Whispering why you'll never grieve me,
Whisper and say that you believe me,
Whispering that I love you,"

phrases that catch in the throat,
rhythms that lift,
melodies that anchor him.

*"Whispering." Song Lyrics by Malvin Schonberger, music by John Schonberger. Vincent Rose may have been a co-composer and Richard Coburn a collaborator on the lyrics. Published 1920 by Sherman, Clay & Co, San Francisco, CA, USA

An Evening with the Syracuse Symphony

> Camille Saint-Saens, "Introduction & Rondo Capriccioso, Op. 28,"
> William Knuth, solo violin

Hundreds of people under the enormous white tent.
Arctic fog settles over Fourth Lake.
Violins have finished tuning up.
The young soloist wipes his brow,
tucks his violin under his chin,
lifts his bow. Fingers want to stiffen.
Sweat beads his forehead.

The conductor begins to dance on his toes, arms
circle empty air, knees bend, body sways.
The young violinist's dark rhythms emerge slowly
soon overcome by a livelier melody.
It circles up from his strings, bounces off elastic
major cords. The loose, whimsical spirit
of the capriccioso escapes his violin
and rises above the orchestra.
Now his fingers dance. His whole body moves—
his face becomes disfigured with torment then ecstasy.

His music ascends leading the orchestra—
a shepherd guiding his flock up a steep slope.
Finally, a climax of arpeggios splinters
the dark sky like a meteor shower.
The conductor's baton holds the night
in a long epiphany of silence.
Then the baton waves like a branch in a storm

and the brass and percussions move in
with thunder and lightning.

The baton sways gently, gently now.
The soloist resumes the lead. Gradual harmonies
untangle the climax. Denouement begins. Peace comes
as stars settle sure light on the tent, and all the strings rejoice
with a low tremble for the young violin virtuoso
who just learned the meaning of transcendence.

View from Aleyska Lodge, Alaska

Windows in a half-circle. Nothing
in the room encloses us
or distracts from the view.
Firs spiral up outside,
stretch to speak
with mountain peaks.
Few birds dare
to dart to these high,
empty spaces. Spires cut deep
into the cerulean silk sky,
transect cotton clouds.
Steep slopes are quilted
in green Irish velvet
and two glaciers lie like great
starched sheets between the shadowy
taffeta of ridges. These moving
beds of ice cover layers
of secret snows marbled and dyed blue
by the centuries. Beneath this summer
still-life an arctic world breathes
and slips toward us
unnoticed, unwarranted.
We feel the power that fingered
the stars in place, registered
our pulse, contained the seas.
We weave ourselves into
this elaborate tapestry, feel connection.
The solitude is not fearsome.

Counting Memories

    for Buddy

Remember how we followed paths through the woods,
built forts, banded songbirds with Dad, searched for wild
flowers and humus for Mother's garden. We turned
summersaults down a honeysuckle-covered hill behind
the Gate House. Holly leaves pricked our bare feet on the path
to the dock. We netted crabs on weighted strings baited with
chicken necks we dropped by the Boat Club pilings. From
the old rowboat we poled for softies and caught tadpoles
in the pond at the top of Harfield Trail.

Every year we trained box turtles to win the Labor Day Turtle Race.
On windy days we watched whirligigs rain over the lawn, and beech
leaves stencil their logo on Dad's new, wet cement. We picked
raspberries and persimmons along Epping Way, listened to cicadae
tune their voices to a sharp, shrill hum. We heard flutes of the thrush
startle evening stillness, and from the upper story branches of the
beech tree the great horned owl haunted our bedtime. When the rains
came, woods became wet, quiet, deep as if fast asleep. Trees wept,
                                    but not us, not us.

Where Nothing Speaks

At sunset the marsh
speaks a language few hear.

Tonight no river otter ripples
the creek's brackish waters
no fish jumps
not even a marsh-hen
fusses from her grassy rooms

but the full moon curls itself on top
of the barren pine like a lemon lollipop

and a deep crimson stripe
unfurls in the sky like a flag

like a wide light in the middle
of a poem where nothing speaks
                      but everything shines.

II. Autumn

You Can Tell It's Fall

by the way the palm fronds clack
upon each other in the wind,

by the way the tallest marsh grasses
scratch the cross planks of the dock,

by the new worry
in the redwing's whistle.

We watch the marsh hen
disappear into the wall of salt grass

then reappear as easily
as the way the good Master

walked right through
a violent crowd

so we can never think of the natural
order of things in the same way again.

Graceful Strings of White Wings

Fall-toned landscape—September in the Arctic,
ice skims. Tundra swans will be leaving fields of snow soon—

We must wait for them.

Their 7-foot wingspan will carry their 15-20 pounds
south on the coattails of the next major cold front.

We must wait at least two months

for these black-billed swans, to migrate in family groups,
sometimes flying three miles high. Soon now, in a blue,
mid-November sky we will hear their wild music.
Then we'll see graceful strings of white wings far in the distance
slipping in lower. Feet spread like landing gear, they will skid down on
our Chesapeake cove—grace on the wing.

Previous stopover, North Dakota, 24 hours, 1,300 miles ago.
Imagine—4,000-5,000 miles since fall in the tundra.
An Odyssey? No—they know their destination.
They come direct—no sidetracks, no diversions.

We wait with buckets of corn.

We will wear the same hat, coat, pants, boots every day
to feed them until they trust us. We sleep
with our windows open to hear their haunting cries.

Listen. I hear them. The swanfall has arrived.
They are repeating nature's ancient directive
another year in our cove, before our eyes—
                              this marvel!

Foxes

I heard them barking last night.
Their high-pitched, gravely yelps
rose above the highest oak and toward
the silent moon—on-going punctuations
in the darkness. A mating call? An alarm?
A fight? A territorial warning?
Who knows their language? I am happy
they are still in the area since they moved
from my woods to hills beyond.
This is a forest—they belong here
with the turtles, owls, black snakes,
the chipmunks, and squirrels.

And their piercing barks belong
to the dark nights of the October moon.

Get Out of My Way

> If ye have faith, and doubt not... ye shall
> say unto this mountain, Be thou removed,
> and be thou cast into the sea; it shall be done.
> *Holy Bible, King James Version, Matthew 21:21*

Today I heard a bag lady sing
as she begged on Bay Street. Cement
walls grew behind her gaunt body.
She paced against their gloomy shadows.
I stood still and listened,
"Jesus said you must obey.
Mountains, get out of my way!"
She repeated the words,
the melody modulated, climbing
a step higher. Her body swayed.
Her rhythms shook the words
from her like wind shakes leaves
from a tree. Every level of her climb
made her more secure, confident,
her mountains would retire.
And I became convinced as I climbed
behind her, up her modulating refrain,
that even if her cup remained
empty when the sun set on her song,
she'd be satisfied, even thankful,
more firm in her faith than ever
that she could not be wrong.

Riding the Bus in New York City

If I lived in New York City,
I'd never read while riding in a bus.
I'd miss seeing the flowers
lining sidewalks and the rush
of traffic, cleaners in their shop windows ironing shirts,
and mannequins wearing the latest tops and short skirts.
I'd miss seeing people relax in sidewalk cafes,
the sky raining confetti on special days,
and vegetables lined up like a Klee painting—
colors merging, new hues.

I couldn't watch beauticians in their shops
cutting curls and painting toes.
I'd never feel the bus lurching to a stop,
Rear brakes grinding out their tunes
like subway turnstiles at noon.
I'd miss the blur of paintings in gallery windows
we'd pass all too soon,
people strolling on Fifth Avenue at lunch hour,
packed shoulder-to-shoulder,
Dog walkers tethered to leashes,
the bravado of cabs and trucks bolder
than lights in Times Square.

You say, "It will soon be the same old scene."
Not in New York City—you will see,
it's not possible to be the same old thing.

My Mother, the Actress

"To her whose heart is my heart's quiet home...
And she my loadstar while I go and come."
    by Christina Rossetti,
      from "Sonnets are full of love, and this my tome"

I was quite young when my mother unpacked a box stored in our basement for years containing her scrapbooks and news clippings, I was in awe, amazed— I never really knew
she was on the stage. She must have trained her lungs early to project to audiences of hundreds, to imitate the voice of a person of any age, male or female, and to speak with the accent
of any nationality. Once she proved her talent to me by taking the parts of all five characters in her one-act play, *The Undercurrent*. She opened her mouth, closed her eyes and lost herself. If I closed my eyes I knew I would loose her. She knew the play by heart. She, only twenty-one had toured the US and Canada with her troupe playing in Vaudeville theatres during the period of silent movies.

Her scrapbook articles that featured the cities in the US and Canada where they performed were full of rave reviews. It was a hit on the Orpheum Circuit, but the Vaudeville acts that followed this early social-protest play had to talk their audiences out of their handkerchiefs and darkness. My mother played Annie, the lead, daughter of a German immigrant whose brutality forced her to the red light district. There was discussion about taking the play to Europe. The year was 1929. With the Great Depression full on, all touring came to a halt.

Mother returned to student life like a princess becoming a commoner. When She entered a classroom she half expected applause. Or when she spoke, she expected silence. She got neither, of course, but she got her degree and taught high school English, drama and speech before she married. More recently, I discovered a treasure in the attic—33 letters she wrote to her parents during her tour. I found more than an itinerary and cities visited—I learned about my mother as a young woman, her interests, her love life, her challenges, her new experiences away from home. A beautiful, free spirit!

Playing and Singing the Old Songs became a Sweet Salve

When my mother passed, my father, in his sadness
and bewilderment, treated himself to an electric home organ—
a big one. It could play twelve accompaniments.
He loved the Big Band, Broadway, March,
Fox Trot, Ballad, and some instrumental arrangements
One problem. Dad could not read a note.
That did not hinder him. He could carry a tune well
and could come up with the one-finger basic melodies
on the keyboard. He worked at it until he memorized
the fingering for many songs—"Blue Skies," "Smile,"
"Whispering," "Blue Velvet," "God Bless the USA,"
and "Tonight, Tonight, I'll See My Love Tonight."
Next he'd switch on his chosen accompaniment—
presto, like magic, he became a performer.
The living room exploded with music.
When guests came, he put on his show.
He played the old tunes everyone knew.
His audience, caught up in his enthusiasm, joined in.
Young friends danced in the middle
of the chamber-in-the-round. The living room
surged with sounds—laughter, shrieks, clapping
to the thumping beat of the bass instrumental undertone,
and his rendition of old favorite melodies.
Guests fussed over him: "How can you do that?"
"When did you learn to play?" "You're amazing!"
A lot of shoulder patting and praise,
kids sat in his lap shouting, "More, more!"

Dad was in his glory. Such evenings relieved what was left of grief.

Memorial Room

    for my brother, Buddy

Your felt hat, the vest with badges, the canteen,
sack of patches, your books and walking sticks.

Dad found them. He collected them.
He arranged them in a memorial room for you.

He added the ice hockey stick, the tennis racquet,
the hubcap, the car radio.

Like the tombs we saw in Cairo— he searched for
everything that brought you pleasure to carry you forward.

Your red row boat moored at the dock
also clings to the memory of your story.

A Visit

Shade of towering white pine.
Smell of hemlock, cedar, spruce.
Green-gifted maples.
Solemn silence except for birdsong.
Time-etched stones, sun-washed.
Chiseled names of ancestors—
weather-burned,
sun-washed, moss-blotched.
Disappearing.
My shadow leans over them.

Getting Through It

> for Diana Der-Hovanessian and
> her poem about a table lit with light

Once I read a poem about a woman
who could not go out in her garden

to pick flowers, so she set her table
with sun-glazed, yellow lemons

for a centerpiece.
When I first learned to mourn,

I thought the blue bowl of heaven
had been shattered. I took the oblong

of an egg and studied it—the heft of it,
its colorless color, its dimensional aspect,

the way it settled into the nest of my hand
until I knew the meaning of potential.

First Lessons

Her looks leaped with laughter
at my silly rhyme.

The child, only two,
digested the meaning,

distinguished sound from sense,
ripped them apart,

condensed them
and recorded her reply

in the book
her laughter wrote

then she responded in time
with a considered retort.

Private Piano Concert

On the other side of the door
our daughter is playing Beethoven,
Brahms, Chopin, Clementi, Khachaturian,
Heller. Her runs are magical.
Her fingers agile and faultless still find
their paths through the tangle of trills.
Chords swirl into the room
rhythms crawl under the door
startle the jasmine-scented air
rest on the new sofa
climb in and out of my memory
raise the dust on years we drove
those long round-trips to piano lessons,
years listening to her daily practice.
Now her melodies settle on my shoulders—
natural, faultless flowing faster
                     and faster,
                                 gathering momentum,
                                         exuberant.

Keeping the Jive

Two sisters dancing,
arms around,
keeping the jive to the Big Band 1930
foxtrot records on the wind-up
phonograph my father left us.
Quick bouncing two-step marks duple time—
their shrieks of laughter resonating through the house.
Living room vibrating under them.
They slow to walking steps, catch their breath.
Music takes over, inspires.
They take up dance positions.
Hands clasped, arms saw the air,
bare feet quicken again to a faster
fox trot. They are transported—
they imagine circling a grand ballroom.

No Ghosts—only a Symphony of Sounds

      for Susan and Richard

The soul of your house is like the architecture of a symphony.
It takes you away—inspires, lifts you, digresses, surprises,
provides ideas, opportunities, relaxation. What was that thud
on the steps? It modulates—changes its mind. You might
have to get used to a new voice, new tone, frightening threats.
What was that moaning sound? Then there might be variations
on the tones—spirited, colorful, serious, dynamic, passionate.
Surprising things happening. Did you hear footsteps in the hall?
                      A house can include all that. Just listen.

It will groan and swear in the wind. Your floors will sing
with creaky voices and your ceiling light will literally
hum you to sleep. The bathroom door will bang open in the middle
of a good dream like a kettle drum, and the *drip, drip, drip*
of the bathtub faucet is a piccolo warming up. Then there's
the surprise rattle and clicking of the ice maker—
                    solo of castanets joining in.

A conspiracy of ghosts?
Did you catch something moving in the corner of your eye?
Their transparency is as deceptive as Hamlet's torments.
Strangers? Share your morning meal with them while
the chair leg cracks under you—a whip in the percussions. Yes,
a house should take you away, but it will always bring you home
                    to the tonic cord.

Never Give Away an Old Dog Dish—

the one down in the basement under the laundry bench
with all the dead crickets and dust in the bottom,

the one used by the stocky, brown Chesapeake Bay Retriever
poisoned by neighbors for his roaming,

the one used by the agile Springer Spaniel who followed
the boy on his paper route,

the one used by the gentle Poodle-Terrier someone
dropped off in the mountains,

the one used by the handsome, black Chow found
roaming the highway at mid-night,

and now, the same one used by the small white & brown
Shih Tzu puppy (unwanted runt of the litter) who lives

to chase squirrels—claiming only the right to his favorite food
in the old dog dish and regular scratching behind the ears.

September Stroll through a Japanese Flower Market

We notice three purple iris
form an isosceles triangle
above a flat dish shaped
like a wide fishing boat.

Petals fold up
like hands
that cup something
solid in air.

Slender green leaves curl
singularly
beside each point
refracting

crystal light
from this perfectly shaped
oriental diamond, floating
in its flat boat

like the boats you saw
moored in the harbor
of Naha, Okinawa—
how your hands folded up

and together like these purple petals
when you heard
the war
had ended.

Lulled to Sleep

It wasn't the distant barking
of wild dogs,
not the low moaning
of the train from Delhi,
nor the smell of smoke from fires
in the small piles of garbage
along the road.

It was the memory of the cows—
horns painted scarlet, green, yellow,
and decorated with ribbons.
Garlands of jasmine around their necks—
the new holy and unrestricted ones,
grazing on roadside garbage.

Their slow meander
enters my dreams.
I am seeking
to lead them home.

The Way Land Invades Sky

I take the path along the ridge,
pick my way through white
Dakota sandstone—loose and flat,
step over exposed jack pine roots.

North, rimrock juts into space
like a peninsula. Great Plains fold east,
merge blue into the horizon.
Horsetooth Reservoir to the south
reflects the gray, omnipotent sky for seven miles.

West, Mummy Mountain curves
like a crescent moon
and scallops north to Laramie.
The Medicine Bows hold land from falling
off the earth the way flying buttresses hold
a cathedral against the heave of heaven.

No one is up, not even deer. No vibration of bird calls.
The dogs pace back and forth, nuzzle my hand,
rub against my leg. It's cold for early fall.
Finally I give in, turn homeward, but I look again:
consider how land invades sky with rimrock, spires,
monuments, and holds back at the same time.

What is it that wants to build a stay
against all this sky?

Rounding Sheep's Meadow

we notice the slant of October sunlight
on the aspen, lingering,
daffodil-yellow against
sea-green ponderosa and fir.
Then we heard them: bugles,
scaling to higher registers
become flute notes
coming from great distances
           echoing,
   answering.

Out of a dusky hillside
figures floated into a clearing.
Bull elk gathered their harems,
           bugling
   closer.

A ritual offered on a great mountain stage:
praise for life renewing itself,
praise for rock and forests,
praise performed on their icy breath,
more ancient than the earliest
           human
   syllable.

Longleaf Pine on the Side of Our House

Our great southern pine looks gaunt in the fall wind.
Trunk grows straight and tall like a ship mast. Branches
angle off high above the house. "Hello. Want us
to take down that dead pine?" The young man
is gaunt too. I see the truck in the street, crew waiting.

I think of my father's march through the Black Forest
as a POW during WW II. He wrote home to Mother
about the trees as if he were their guest.
All that dense, dark beauty captured him. He returned
to Germany forty years later. Visited the Black Forest.
"Hardly a tree left," he wrote Mother, "old ones cut.
They've reforested—all mostly young trees."

"That tree, dead?" I say to the young man.
"You should have seen it in the last hurricane. It bent over
like a giraffe grazing on acacia. It swayed in the wind,
combed electric air. It beat the voice out of the storm.
It danced. No sir, not our pine tree. It's full of life.
                              Thanks anyway."

A Comparison

Fog over the cove rolls
out toward the river as sunrise deepens
to scarlet, turns
to crimson, dissolves
to mauve.
Horizon of trees reflect
leafless branches on the placid water.
Erased by night, objects come
into focus again—boathouses, docks,
sailboats, buoys drifting on their tethers.
Houses on the hills emerge more slowly.
And you, standing there by the chair,
                changeless, constant.

III. Winter

New Reality

Early morning, consider
how hoar frost
creates cut glass shapes.
You think you must be walking
through the Steuben Glass factory.

Late afternoon, consider
how hoar frost still
swaddles fallow fields,
corn stalks, branches, buds,
bushes, tree trunks. It casts
a gray glow like fog
settling in to stay the night.

Consider the grotesque
shapes at dusk, suggesting
the fearsome and the humorous
the way imagination
can distort our days.

Into Winter Wind

Six white ibis cluster on salt stained
planks where the dock widens.
They are resting as falling sun paints sky lapis,
crimson-brushed, then coral and magenta
with strains of amethyst. Windows
in the homes along Greenfield Creek glow
like hot coals. The ibis preen and stretch
before they will ride the west wind
into the deepening purple-tinged sky
toward their rookery.
Little blue herons pass over them,
great egrets have already gone, anhingas
fly south, parallel to the water's surface
toward St. John's River. I am a motionless
tree on their sawgrass horizon. I break the old
winter wind. Marsh water beneath me
glints fire. In their own time all six ibis rise
as of one mind, cross to the other side of the dock.
On black tips they lift into deepening light
and paper the sky with white wings.
I am witness.   I am washed
                             and I come seeing.

Orchestra-in-the-Round

Out on the dock
we stand in the middle
of owl music. The low
bleating monosyllabic succession:
   who-who-who-awwwah
chisels the night air
here, there.
         No, over there.

Answers. Not echoes. Like
Greek choral singers,
they throw out their own
variations for wind
to stretch over water
through darkness
over hills and longleaf pines,
over scratching salt grasses
accompanied by stringed cicadas,
tympani of splashes, squawking
horns of marsh-hens.
         Enter owls again.

Not theatre-in-the-round.
An orchestra surrounds us
even when we take the silver path
the moon makes back to shore, even
when we sit inside, still
              included in owl music.

Direction

This tall, glass bird feeder,
a silo for seeds,
dangles on a long wire
from a high branch
of the live oak.

Last night it thrashed
in the storm, glass reflecting
clouded full-moon
and lightning flashes. Lantern-
like it swayed, tossed
in wind currents and electric air.
Through the night we watched

this torch, testament
to the wind's direction,
its power.   Today birds congregate
in steady rain for soaked kernels
and a still perch. Cardinals in trees
click and chirrup to set

their position for their mates.
Our binoculars cannot pick them
out of the oak
until a red jet lands on the feeder,
catches his image in glass,
selects a seed, sets his own direction
as the child sleeping upstairs
dreams of doing.

Up Harfield Trail to Robinhood Road

From the trail, we see houses clinging
to the sides of ravines, ascending the steep hills.
At night their lights stairstep into the dark sky
like constellations collecting themselves.
Through leafless branches of birches, oaks,
poplars, windows blink and glow amid chimney smoke,
smolder like hot coals in the cold air, merge
with other stars so we can't tell house lights
from starlight. We cannot touch their heat even if
we reach out, but they connect us to whatever
is out there. Let's invent new constellations—
Little Owl, Big Owl, Snapping Turtle,
Barking Fox, and welcome them to our universe
of blinking families—shapes of the familiar
to guide us at night like the constellations
Odysseus used to find his way home from Troy.

.

Observation

She loves the chime true crystal water glasses make
when she taps them with her silver spoon, but she likes
watching, through her binoculars, scenes
from her window even more. She can understand

why a pair of great blue herons flies into the cove once a day.
She watches them fish the low tide mud flats
below the tamaracks or look for sun fish around the pilings.
Here large birds can escape the elements, the noisy fishermen
and boaters. They guard their solitude—as she guards hers.

When the woods are gray and heavy with snow-smoke
and icicles hang on spruce tips like glass ornaments,
she watches ruddy ducks fly across the frozen cove
in steady rhythm, land in open water and bob
like white buoys in the currents from the river.
They line up on the edge of the ice to sleep—a temptation
for foxes that brave thin crusts to get to them at night.

She has escaped the elements. Her life no longer
asks questions—it answers them: true-toned,
intuitive, clear like her crystal chimes.

Audience

Today the winter seashore is shaped in rivulets—
a washboard, invaded by warm sea pools
fed by ocean streams. The laughing gulls
with their black heads are back.
Their rollicking calls echo down the beach.
They soar, some dive into the waves

for the daily catch or they search the beach
for shell fish. Just as day drops lower
on the horizon, they congregate into one
large flock and settle on a flat sandy stretch.
All face south gathering energy from the last,
warm rays of sun. Dressed identically,
they are like choral performers

absorbed in the rhythmic undulations
and booming voice of the speaker—that voice
of wave upon wave upon the sand, resolute, hypnotic,
inescapable sound of pounding—
the voice of the source of their daily sustenance
providing just enough for one day at a time.

Iroquois Lodge

The way my father told it, I can see my grandparents and great grandfather crossing iced-over Fourth Lake to Gingerbread Point on snowshoes to look at property. Grandmother probably wore layers under her long, black, wool dress and coat, her shoulders and head bundled in scarves. They bought the property about 1903. Great grandfather (a retired carriage manufacturer) built a camp for them to host summer vacationers. There must have been 50 rocking chairs on the three stories of wrap-around porches when Dad took us there to spend his vacation. In the old Adirondack lean-to on the rocks by the lake, my parents sang old camp songs with neighbors by a roaring campfire. Through my open window, I heard their voices circling up with the smoke.

We children played in a sandbox, swam at our secret beach, and the mail boat delivered our mail every day and picked up outgoing letters. My grandmother boarded the Pickle Boat to buy her groceries. We visited the town dump on our parents' shoulders to see the black bears and we climbed Bald Mountain. A few old white wood hotels remained on the lake—a glad remnant from the Gilded Age. We spent many summers there until my grandmother sold the Lodge. It was torn down, replaced with a modern, gentrified structure. That too was torn down recently—replaced with a woodland camp recalling the charm of my grandparents' Iroquois Lodge. Loons call, a merganser family coasts the shoreline. Under the moon the lake still wears a silver skin.

We Had Almost Forgotten How

mountains are illumined by winter sunset
and foothills blur into a hazy charcoal mist.

Tents of blue spruce and balsam circle
the lake above turn-of-the-century lodges.

We smell wood smoke rising in cold,
pine-dusted air and hear the muted wail

of a loon claiming her territory—a descant
above the settling melodies at dusk.

"Mamma, the mountains are chasing us!"
our daughter cries as we drive west.

Stories rise from this landscape
about lumbermen, abundant wildlife,

new railroads, guides, traders, the grand hotels
and camps—stories we cannot forget because

they follow us like these mountains chasing us.
They are imprinted on our memory—a heritage
                                      we gladly accept.

Inherited

Passed down, folded in the small trunk from Holland,
forgotten, attic-preserved over sixty years.
This quilt covers us now with centenarian warmth.
Hand stitches, small, and as regular
as any sewing machine. Strong threads hold together
a geometry of red and white checks as precise
as the quilted fields outside town. Now it inspires
the landscape of our room—
        comforts us.

Consider the patience of that thimble finger,
her wish to make something useful and lovely,
her precision of mind alert to balance and form.
Theme and variation inhabit the design
as in classical music. Her story speaks through line,
structure, balance of color, an eye for composition.
It will stay our lives.
        It votes for all that is human, original.

We've inherited an art form that suggests the immortal.
An ancestor's gift—we've always had it and will pass it on.
We lie awake smelling the faintness of muslin
from earth's flax and red dye from secret
German formulas. We fall asleep under beauty
that cannot recall its creator,
        avoids its own name.

Snowbound

Foreboding sky. Gray, ominous, no horizon.
A sudden multitude of birds on the feeder
then night steals color from the world
and the silhouettes of trees bend and toss
with solitary dignity—an accurate forecast.

On the opposite bank of Saltworks Creek
a road rides the hills gently, visible now
through leafless winter trees. Headlights probe
the dark. Cars carry extra water, firewood,
some necessary groceries.

Before dawn no headlights search for the road.
The fire-red orb of day opens a jeweled box.
Trees wear diamonds—landscape
all a-dazzle. The red flash of the cardinal
on the feeder ignites white morning.
Let day cast this original light
over our shoulders for a sign.

Faces in the Door

Snowfalls were frequent that winter. Wet, heavy, fluffy. School closings became so common children grew tired of sledding and building snowmen in the back yard. "We could build an igloo," someone suggested. "How can we do that; where can we get ice blocks?" One of them started rolling large snowballs, arranged them in a circle, leaving an open space—a door. They piled more snowballs on top. Heavy to lift up. Mom and Dad helped. A third row, this time, tilting the balls in slightly, curving the walls inward until the last row almost met at the top. One final snowball closed it off. The wet snow stuck together.

They were Eskimos! They had built a house of snow. They could even stand up in it. It took several trips to carry pillows, sleeping bags, books, and snacks into their cozy igloo The sun dropped over the snow-blurred horizon of trees. Mom and Dad brought pizza, hot chocolate, and a lantern. The temperature dropped, the igloo turned to ice. Four dark silhouettes appeared inside the lighted globe. They were snug, warm and so satisfied with themselves. From the illumined doorway, their faces peered out now and then to check on the moon, the stars, the hooting owl, and the faces in the kitchen window.

Why Take a Photo of an Old Goat House

The realtor—a very savvy salesman—sold the cottage with the fishbowl view of Saltworks Creek to my parents. All he needed to say was, "You know there's an old goat house up on the hill that could be made into charming playhouse." That got my immediate attention and my mother's imagination. We all tromped up the hill through four inches of snow. The weathered old house had a high slanted ceiling with a loft. It just needed cleaning and painting.

First Mother borrowed the neighbor's hose and used lye to clean the house. Next came whitewash for the walls, linoleum floorcovering, some furnishings—rocking chair, old cot, table and chairs, a little cabinet, old hook rug over the linoleum. We put up curtains, lined the two windows with jars of ivy, nailed up some pictures. We were the original *Boxcar Children*. It became the playhouse and clubhouse of the neighborhood. The woods all around hummed with bird song, turtles roamed, raccoons and squirrels explored the high branches. Wildflowers flourished—bloodroot, Dutchman's breeches, snowdrops, lady-slipper, violets.

It never occurred to anyone to take a photo even when they tore it down. Expansion, convenience, clean up the hill, make room for a garage—that old goat house is not used anymore. In my mind, it's still there somewhere along the deer path that rambles up through the mature forest—tulip poplar, beech, hickory— those giants that now reign with ivy covering their feet, the hillside, and the goathouse foundation. Where imagination created it, memory must keep it.

Your Nourishing

Snow was still frozen into round silver coins
on top of holly leaves the morning robins flocked
by the hundreds to eat the just-ripe red berries.
We listened to the excited chorus
of chirping, cheeping, and contented peeping.
You photographed them as they darted
and fluttered from branch, to higher limb,
to sagging end twigs where they teetered and swayed.
"There...over there to the right," I pointed
as your camera focused, clicked,
clicked again ... again. You recorded
their winter colors and bulging red bellies.

I think about your husbanding that nourished me.
I remain to record it.

The Purpose

How beautifully
the pink camellia rosettes
unwind their buds in winter
and sit on their waxy branches
like ornaments on a gown.

I would no more pick them
than claim another's poem.
I would no more change them
for another flower
than change the course of the river.

They have been born in January
to call back the humming bird
to call back the painted bunting
to call me from my sheaf of words
to look again.

IV. Spring

Forecasts

Ice sheets on the river have only begun to crack
and break apart. The unquestionable
announcement—a ringing, raspy salute,
oak-ar-ree, comes from the redwings perched among
the still-red rose hips bordering the salt marsh.
We are startled out of our winter depths
by this first impulsive prediction—their exuberance
comparable only to the western meadowlarks
we used to hear calling from fence posts,
their eager flutes bubbling out over the field
at dawn even before the prairie grasses
had broken out of their icy straight-jackets.

What is it they see? Perhaps it could lift our spirits
with the same quick pulse of expectancy.

The Chuck-Will's-Widow,

the first voice of spring, whistles
his distinct southern phrase

over the marsh like a boy casting
for mullet, and after reeling it in

slowly
for effect

the bird casts again
and again. From the creek's

headwaters, far in the distance,
his answer travels to him.

Late into night we hear the bird
casting and reeling in

casting and reeling in
until his song and its answer

trail off in unison like love
riding tonight on the air between us.

A Wet May Morning

We see trees bend with the weight of rain
and the memory of last night's wind.
In the afternoon sun, they will forget
the storm and lift themselves again,
regain their height,
regain their healthy will.
Against this tablecloth
of a wet May morning,
yellow daffodils shrivel in their old skin
and purple lilacs curl at the tips.
But tulips have opened like poppies
and march in columns, four-abreast

in parade colors—hemlocks and oaks
still spreading their skirts over them.

Reward

Today out on the dock
I felt pinned to the cool blue
of the stretching sky.
Brown grasses bend into archways
by the inaudible whip of the wind.
But this was my reward—
four bluebirds flew across the wide creek,
passed six inches from my shoulder
as if I didn't exist.
Azure-toned wings caught the sun's spotlight
as they banked leeward.
I heard their cheerful twitter
and knew instantly
I could translate it.

Our Walks

The dogs and I loved
our morning walks along
the red sandstone paths
to the outcropping of rocks
scalloped like the humpback
of a dinosaur, Horsetooth Reservoir
stretching its mirror for seven miles
below us. Cows wandering,
their rusty bells rattling. Some cactus.

The hiss of colored, hot air balloons,
rising also with strong spring gusts
over the next hill, startled us.
We'd return home
red-dust-covered head to foot.
Not in any hurry to shake it off.

June First

We would settle here
hope-down among
rotting roots, tubers,
layers of oak leaves,
new fiddleheads unwinding,
acorn caps. Another chance.

Our woods out back bogs in low places.
Mosquitoes practice their low humid-hum.
Expectancy in the blue jay's sermon,
rejoicing in the flutes of thrushes.

Song-blue light of afternoon
filters through yellow pine brushes,
lady slippers conquer high places.
One is white like this new-found feeling
we can call home.

"Hello Susan," I Said to You

That's how it always begins—
with a name:
lily-of-the-valley
Wakefield Avenue
Port Washington
May
Long Island.
Place names, proper names—
what we call identity—
like the sound of a voice
on the phone
that one recognizes instantly
as I recognized you by name
without hesitation and called for you
again and again as nurses punched in
my stomach in that square, sterilized room
where pure, white fragrance
of lily-of-the-valley celebrated
the chaste, new breath.

More than Déjà-vu

Morning began for me with the twitter
and flittering flight of four goldfinches high
in the mimosa blossoms.
Their design was the bird feeder
where the squirrel hung up-side down.

Such spirited song shaped the day to pencil-
point sharpness. Time between was suspended—
You all were there again—Dad
in his La-Z-Boy rocker, Brother reading,
Mother at the window looking out.

Shower of light washing and rinsing
the scene—goldfinches still hovering,
mimosa shivering with sudden luminosity.

All These Comings and Sudden Goings

                    A large flock
of black-masked raiders descended
on our dogwood tree. They thought
their masks hid them, but I heard their munching,
happy peeping, and fluttering.

                    No one could miss the clutter
of so many cedar waxwings feasting on one small tree.
Then all merriment stopped, and the sky was filled
with one note—the highest tone I'd ever heard—
like thousands of tiny bells

                          ringing in unison.
There was a whooshing like a sudden wind,
then the sky was as silent as a closet
and the tree was as barren as the night
my mother disappeared with her last breath.

                    I heard the high note
of a bird usher her to the other side of light.
Years pass. How could one prove they were ever here?
Memory must uphold reality.
It is a burden nothing else can bear.

Sophie's Painting

A rainbow—
she painted it for me on a piece
of cardboard when her grandfather
passed suddenly.
She wrote on the back:
> Dear Grammy. I love you.
> Always stay up with the rainbows.
> Lots of love, Sophie

She wanted to climb higher.
She wanted me to join her.
I had no choice.

"Way Down Upon the Swanee (sic) River"

for Tom, Fay, and John

It was the year we got locked in the wildlife refuge at Okefenokee. We rested at the top of the lookout tower, boggy plain below, sun slipping lower. No sandhill cranes visible. We saw a few on our way in. They say thousands massed here a few years ago and took off for Canada and Siberia. A few stretches of water mirrored the drain of deep vermillion from the horizon. Then landscape fell into sudden shadows and darkness. A ranger had to unlock the gate for us. "Too early for any staging yet. Maybe next week…or the next. Depends on the weather and the up-drafts, the water level too," he said. "The birds decide in this Suwanee* River watershed. They've been using this flyway every year since the beginning of time." He added, "Don't expect any changes now." A coincidence—we were near the Stephen C. Foster State Park so named to remember his folksongs based in this area. I sang them over and over in grade school—drawn to those truly All-American lyrics and melodies, not borrowed from another nation or brought over. And they've survived—same elastic fabric of imperishability as these sandhill cranes.

---

* Despite the spelling of the river in the title of this song, written by Stephen Foster, the actual spelling of the river is *Suwanee*. It flows in the US from Georgia and through Florida to the Gulf of Mexico.

Like Love in the Afternoon

I hear the syncopation of rain
on my attic roof
downpour of kettle drums
celebration of timpani (more
than a symphony's worth),
windy whistling in drainpipes.
Cisterns, wells, aquifers, overflowing.
End of a season's dearth,
quenching thirst. You are here now:
the empty heart is full again.

Perfect Camouflage

Snap of a twig, a closer look into the tropical
undergrowth. Leafy cloak of foliage, emerald colored
and honey-toned, lifted on a pair of purple gallinules foraging
among the colorful leaves and reeds in a sun-dusted patch of light—

the same colors on the birds dispelled the gloom
from upper story pines and palmettos. The surprise
of prismatic tones played with each other. Feathers dazzled
with indigo hues, the greens and blues of turquois,

a translucence more lustrous than the tones on a dove's neck
or on the wings of a crow. The male carried an ultra-blue plate
on his head like a shield. A red beak was his sharp sword.
Bright yellow legs and feet—long and agile—propelled him

through the muck and tangle of the watery marsh. I can imagine
Monet would have loved to paint these New World rails.
Such a sudden glimpse of moving color might excite
his interest as surely as morning light on flowers at Giverny.

The unexpected, the colorful, the delight of discovery.
The way light ignites.

Black Sleeve of Night

When light slips into the black sleeve of night,
when darkness steals color from flowers and trees,
then silhouettes of longleaf pines will toss in the wind,
and squawking of marsh hens will cease.
It is the time of the bats. I see them dart
and swerve over open water. Once in Costa Rica
I held a small brown bat in my two hands.
Soft warm body twisted and squirmed—a collection
of yearnings and impulses—
preference for the night like the owls
or great cats that see with other seeing,
little comprehended by those who cherish the light.

Symbiosis

The wisteria vines covering the bank
never bloom, but those at the shoreline persist.
They have coiled themselves to the top
of the old tamarack tree Dad planted fifty years ago.
There they can achieve their purpose—
crown the tree with royal colored blossoms
that hang like exotic fruit. What is there to resist?
The tamarack is glad to support them.
He is a gracious host. He senses their need to flower
by hanging from something, and he, so distinguished,
can claim a dual nature—his limbs
tangled with gentle lavender vestibules of color.
The flowers perfectly disguise his true identity if only
for the few weeks while the blossoms exist.
That is enough glory for an old tree to bear
                                        in one year.

Flutes of the Wood Thrush

for Grace and Sophie

Your practiced eyes will see
a moving bird
and ask, "What is its name."

Highest melody will fall
on your quick ears—
every dusk the same.

Soon you'll recognize the call—
the ordered syllables, the ascending flute,
the echo that will remain.

Your eyes, your ears must remember all—
the fair and melodious bird and song,
and you will pass its name and message on.

V. Ekphrasis Poems

What Is Ekphrasis Poetry?

Ancient Greeks applied the term *ekphrasis* to poems that describe a work of art—painting, sculpture, porcelain, literature, and today the list includes photography. An early example of ekphrastic poetry can be found in *The Iliad* in which Homer describes Achilles' shield at length.

Over the centuries, poets have enlarged the definition of *ekphrasis* to include a type of interpretation or meditation in which the poet seeks to present more than a mere description of the piece of art. The poet might interpret the symbolism, or present relationships or connections. The poet may integrate historical background, or imagine what the artist is depicting. The poet may wish to draw comparisons.

Some famous ekphractic poems include: "Ode on a Grecian Urn" by John Keats, "My Last Duchess" by Robert Browning, "The Starry Night" by Anne Sexton, "Landscape with the Fall of Icarus" by William Carlos Williams, "Nine Nectarines and Other Porcelain" by Marianne Moore.

See: *The Oxford Companion to English Literature*, Seventh Edition, edited by Dinah Birch, Oxford University Press, 2009, Oxford, UK.

What Ghiberti Knew

>A 21 x 17 1/2 guilt bronze quatrefoil, "Sacrifice of Isaac"
>by Lorenzo Ghiberti, won the 1401 competition for
>the north doors of the Cathedral Baptistry at Florence

The ram caught by his horns in a thicket
twists dimensionally upon the mountain.

The servants and the saddled ass wait below
cast in the left side of the diagonal.

Isaac kneels like a Hellenistic statue
upon the wood, upon the altar.

Abraham, sculpted in relief,
has stretched forth his arm.

The shadow it leaves shows
the depths despair will forge.

In his hand, his knife, the position,
the purpose, the grief in the purpose.

Light gilts the blade,
the sharp point. Ghiberti

gives us this moment of climax
when the point of action intersects

the point of rock-rigid faith. Abraham's
son, the son of prophesy, the son

of promise is to be the sacrificed.
It is at this precise moment

the angel flies into the intersection
in foreshortened relief from flat

space above their heads and calls to him,
Abraham, Abraham. It is at this very point

of mental incision into Abraham's
heart just before the angel commands,

Lay not thine hand upon the lad, that the blade
becomes the conduit to a new conception

of one God for this tribal patriarch.   Ghiberti knew
that when Abraham took it in, the lesson

in full relief was about love,
about the sacrifice of self and nothing else.

The Mozart Sonata

    after Berthe Morisot, 1894

She painted them
        while they played—
daughter Julie, on the violin
        accompanying Morisot's niece
Jeannie, on the piano.
        Was it the music
or the artist that colored
        the parlor with light?
The girls bend over their instruments
        so naturally we forget
the artist calculates her effect
        with broad, loose brushstrokes.
She paints her figures as they lean into the tremble
        of their parallel trill.
Morisot lets us feel Julie's
        slight deference
to Jeannie by the way she bends over the chest
        of her instrument.
The artist's pastel palette lifts the scene. We can feel
        the joy of nimble fingers—
cousins converging in a harmony so seamless
        it resonates until
the power of the sound fills the room—
        saffron energy
swirling us into the scene until we hear
        its tremolo buffet the walls
like the clamoring of morning birds.

Irises

    after Vincent Van Gogh, 1889

All intensities of the color blue—of sky,
of water, of the opalescence of a crows wing.
The large orchid-like statements about life—
bulbous & full. Constructs of tissuey
organza and silk petals,
delicate & tough, circling bold, yellow stamens.
Contrast the stems and leaves—the dark spears.
Green iridescence of tropical birds,
wings pointed, held outright, ready
to fly. The flowers grow
from the deep, red soil
of Van Gogh's native seeing, not
from the parched ground
in the garden asylum at St. Remy
where each year
the irises multiplied. The artist
noticed how they grew
                out of the shadows.

Over My Shoulder

> After de Goya's *Red Boy*. Portrait of a small boy,
> Don Manuel Osorio Manrique de Zuniga, 1784-1792

The magpie with a string tied to its leg,
the finches in the domed cage, and the three cats
ready to pounce on the magpie are all symbols, of course,
not the usual toys for a small boy, but I had to use them—
I have something to say about Don Manuel.

His father, Count Altamira, opened his grief to me
like a sorrowful letter after his small son
passed away. I did not seek the commission
to paint this portrait of his child from memory,
but I am a father also and I've known

the same a terrible loss more than once.
I painted the boy in a scarlet, Turkish-styled suit.
Nothing could contrast the subject more against my pallet
of soft-toned sables. I've trimmed his outfit
with a silk sash and a flouncy, wide bow,

a matching lace collar and satin shoes.
I want to make this child immortal.
I'm working on his pale face at the moment.
The neck emerges from the collar, his head
and shoulders penetrate the luminous right diagonal

of my canvas, but his right arm and hand stretch into the dark corner
of the left diagonal. You understand
what I am suggesting here and how it fills me with sadness—
I can hardly work at times. His hair, the color of horse chestnuts,
matches his eyes. He's not worried

about the cats and his pet bird. He's looking over my shoulder.
Something attracts his attention through the window.
Even if I could follow his gaze, I could not see
what he's looking at. He is seeing beyond seeing.
He knows something about the light.

The Color of His Language

I and the Village, Marc Chagall, 1911

In Paris he seeks a refuge.
He cannot name the flowers, birds, trees.
The new foreign words are sweet to the tongue,
but he cannot produce even a street name.
He speaks in his original language
of color from his bright palette.
Memory of his homeland.
fills his canvasses with icons
and the star of David, roosters and scythes,
white lambs and blue goats, green faces.
He tells of lovers and circuses,
 peasants dancing on rooftops.

Yes, he defies some laws.
    Perspective.   Gravity.
So do the dancers at the Ballet of Paris
whose elevations soar like ecstatic swallows.
His color stories speak
more than fantasy, they show us
the country of his native seeing
where he returns again and again—
where anyone can carry a lamb
over the moon.

They Think I'm Deaf

Beethoven's *Choral Symphony No. 9 in D minor, Op. 125,* 1884

Sudden, as a winter night arrives,
a conductor lifts his baton.
I am sitting in the front row.
Since I'm deaf, I've never heard
my symphony performed,
and I will not tonight. But I will follow it
reliving the melody as I sit
amid notes and tones as if among stars,
fitting them into their proper orbits.

Melodies blend and flow into phrases, and
I feel them gather to a climax. The tumult
becomes deafening (even to me). It shakes
this concert chamber, the universe utterly.
Just at the crisis, dawn breaks,
my Ode to Joy delivers the healing answer.
Tones retreat until they hover,
whispering.

The orchestra stops when notes
return to their reservoir
in silence. Performers bow
to the ebb and flow of applause
and leave the chamber.

This performance will fade
into its place in memory
as this night will merge

into the next dawn,
and the sea into the land,
the land into the sky.

But I who hear no instrument,
go out arranging sound in endless
combinations as I walk. These
I hear as starlight is heard.

In Jan Van Eyck's
Portrait of Arnolfini and His Wife,

       Oil on oak, National Gallery, 1434.
           For my dog, Dancer

the dog stands erect, posing, fur is trimmed and coiffed.
My dog, Dancer's fur is shaggy, covers her ears in tangles
and falls disheveled over her paws.

The eyes of Arnolfini's dog are as vacant as cloudy
night skies, Dancer's eyes sparkle,
like the moon and stars.

The ears of Arnolfini's dog point like two triangles
glued to his head. Dancer's fold down and cock
forward to catch the slightest sound.

The dog in the portrait stands at attention, moves by decree.
Dancer bows and stretches, sprawls at my side,
yawns into relaxation.

She is always ready to jump up and follow. She responds
to my whisper as if she knows what I am thinking before
words form on the crust of air between us.

Pregnant Woman

    after Marc Chagall's painting, 1913

The woman standing stories tall
like a skyscraper is pregnant
with a grown man centered inside her.
Many of Chagall's pantheon
are present here—a white goat climbs
into the crimson clouds,
peasant houses stand upright,
a disembodied half-face smiles,
and the man with the ox plows
into the clouds. A fingernail moon rides
toward the woman's shoulder,
and four birds soar above the horizon
which fills in for the otherwise ubiquitous violin.

The woman stands on the horizon of the world—
red clouds form the geometry of her praise.
Her face is the green of emeralds,
of spring forests, of lawns
sleeping in the slant of an afternoon sun.
She listens. Her left foot taps.
This must be true for where there are birds, there is music.

To hear what she hears,
to see what she sees.

A Painting for Bella, My Fiancée, My Love

    after *The Birthday* by Marc Chagall, 1915
    Museum of Modern Art, New York, NY

Ah, Bella, you've come with flowers for my birthday.
No, don't put them in a vase just now. Let me find
a fresh canvas for my easel. I must capture this moment.
Don't move Dearest! Here now, I'm back.
I'll just set this up. First I'll use great lyrical strokes—
the gray-blue of early dusk, brown of a doe's coat,
deepest orange, lots of black and white.
My colors will rival the Fauves.

My forms must plunge us into the sudden rapture
of this moment. You, Bella, will lift off the floor
with the exuberance of my touch.
Now I'll paint myself lifting up, up, up over you,
my body twisting into an impossible curve, reaching,
stretching my neck to kiss you, contorting myself
painfully like the figures in Expressionist paintings.
What else can confess the weightless feeling of my love?
You will see my passion in the wanton green
of my shirt. This painting will be my ode to our love.
Now I think I'll flatten our forms in Cubists style.

Of course, I'll let lumiérè-liberté of the Impressionists
flood my canvass. As you can tell, I have no use for surface
appearances. My perspectives must defy common logic.
I'll have nothing to do with the ordinary sequence of time,
and especially gravity—nothing can pull us from this pinnacle.
No walls or space can confine the freedom

of our love. Don't you feel the sheer ecstasy of it all—
the floating sensation? I am next to you.
It's not a dream. What is real is what you are feeling!
The moment is ours. Your flowers, the birthday tarts
and tea on the buffet can wait.

Woman II, 1961

> After the Abstract Expressionist painting
> by Willem de Kooning. Oil on paper mounted on canvas.
> The Haskell Collection, Jacksonville, FL

I sit here admiring you as you gaze out at me through
cold-toned sadness. You tower in the center
of your canvas-room like a mysterious bird that can't fly.
But would you fly if you could?

I think not. There is color—a hint of some shine left behind
the wash of pinky beiges that conceal you like a veil.
Blue becomes you, Dear, and the yellows stabilize you.
They suggest a boldness about you I've long admired.
It can't be covered, but it's not enough to lift you up.
It's the heavy reds that degenerate to brown that worry me.
They cloak you like a shroud. You are cowering. Why?
Whatever is scorched on your mind, like Hester's *A* hanging
around her neck, is not unredeemable. Do you really wish
to recede toward the open spaces and disintegrate
at the sight of me? Death is never the answer.

You know your grimaces make me nervous, and your energy
is dissolving before my eyes like a genie going back
into her bottle. Don't go! Don't get me wrong—
I know how the years can bring on a momentum
of hard things not nice gifts neatly wrapped up
for a birthday present. Tell me what troubles you.
The world gets thrown at all of us, you know.
I chose to hang you on my wall, and there you'll stay.
You must find some stability in that. I'm not prepared
to look at the end of space without you, so let's relax a little.
Now don't go, I haven't finished my point.

I'm trying to help you. Wouldn't you rather sit with me and watch
the moon from the window, gathering its constellations
into a grand congregation instead of hiding there on your canvas
behind that veil of strong, transparent washes? Yes, your structure is a bit
ambiguous, but mystery challenges me,
and honestly, Dear, I love your yellow stockings.

Mysterious Women

>   after Edgar Degas' *Women Combing Their Hair, ca.1875-76*
>   Oil on paper mounted on canvas.

The three women at the beach could be sisters,
or they could be three sketches of the same woman.
Degas permits us to see only one of their faces,
but we notice that their white muslin dresses
are not exactly the same. This secures
their individual identities and cancels one mystery.
A first glance reveals their total self-absorption.

The woman standing has positioned herself
for command. She looks sideways distractedly,
her gaze following the slight tilt of her head
as she combs her long, brunette hair flat
and down covering the side of her face.
There is no pull in her comb. Her body merges
into the waves behind her, into the sand under her.
Her private thoughts follow her wistful gaze inland.

The middle woman has thrown her hair over the front
of her head, holding it at the crown with her left hand.
With close-eyed concentration she combs from the back,
forward and down covering most of her face with her arm.
Her beach dress reveals the sensual curvature
of her back. We can imagine she winces as the comb
pulls the tangles down and out.

The woman sitting in the sand tugs at her hair
with her comb. We see most of her face. Her eyes

are also closed. She is doubled over with effort
and with the stress of the comb pulling
at her long auburn hair that falls like a horse's mane
into her lap. Her dress is falling off her shoulder
revealing full breasts under the lace bodice.

The women have no interest in chatting, confiding,
light gossip. Degas, the master of revelatory gesture, gives us
no ordinary sunbathers. Their gestures admit they
have withdrawn into a sacred privacy—they will bear
no interruption nor heed any distraction.
They must be retreating to prepare
for something extraordinary. They sift their thoughts
like children sift sand. Perhaps they must fulfill
a covenant they made in some wilderness moment
and they imagine ancient times and places—
the story of the Magdalene preparing herself worthy
of Him, ready to wash his feet with her long hair.

Ode on a Wedgewood Teapot

    Jasperware, Hanley in Staffordshire, 1766

There is a garden. A small child plays a flute,
a lady blows her horn, her gown billows in the wind.
A queen sits on a bench, watches. Someone brings her fruit.

Turn the teapot. A couple stands under a tree.
Night-blue tones glow through their vitreous shapes.
The chaperone, the color of old, white marble,
looks the other way, and a cupid will soon lift
into azure-toned air.

The child, the lady and the queen
are waiting for the couple and their chaperone
to come before the queen for her blessing.

A Sylvan scene persists in this memorial to beauty
told on my Jasperware teapot in my china cabinet,
passed on to me through the generations.
It is not the useful handle and spout I notice,
but the bowl shape, the perfect circle

and the luminous, before-nightfall dye, unglazed,
with the fine-white relief of vitreous stoneware
illumining its dark body. To answer your question,
John Keats, *What leaf-fringed legend*
haunts about thy shape...?*

There is no serpent here, nor a forbidden tree.
The Queen will always be there waiting.
Simple truth set the perfect scene outside Time.
The historian makes seven days a symbol of completeness.
But the beauty, the immortality of the potter's art
                                    must also teach us.

*From "Ode on a Grecian Urn" *by John Keats*

Notes about the Author

Bonny Barry Sanders was born in Dover, Delaware, raised and educated in Annapolis, MD, and received her BA from Principia College, her MA from Arizona State University, and her MFA from Colorado State University. She has taught English composition, humanities, and writing workshops at several universities.

Ms. Sanders is the author of two collections of poems, *Touching Shadows* (2005) and *October House* (2016), and an historical fiction *Kiss Me Good-bye* (2007). Her play *Schoolmaster from Flat Creek* (1990) was produced at the University of New England. Beginning in 1987, her poems began appearing in magazines, literary periodical and anthologies including *The South Carolina Review*, *Birmingham Poetry Review*, *Louisiana Literature*, *The Florida Review*, *The Midwest Quarterly*, *Plainsongs*, *South Dakota Review*, *Louisiana Review*, *The Christian Science Monitor*, *Blueline*, *Connecticut Review*, and many others. She is also the author of published articles, book reviews, and children's stories. She won the Royal Palm Literary Award for Poetry, a grant from the Community Foundation of Northern Florida, and was the honored recipient of two three-week residencies at The Atlantic Center for the Arts (1999 and 2000). For ten years, she served as an editorial reader for *Kalliope: A Journal of Women's Literature & Art*

Ms. Sanders has lived in many states and traveled abroad, which she says, have provided a rich and valuable resource for her writing and have inspired many of her poems. At present she divides her year between living in Jacksonville, FL and at Wren's Nest Cottage in Annapolis, MD where she grew up. She also enjoys many trips to Princeton, NJ to visit her family.

Made in the USA
Columbia, SC
09 December 2023